THE ART OF COMMERCIAL DRUMMING

THE ART OF COMMERCIAL DRUMMING
HOW TO DEVELOP A SOLID GROOVE AND BECOME A POCKET DRUMMER

iUniverse books may be ordered through booksellers or by contacting:

iUniverse
1663 Liberty Drive
Bloomington, IN 47403
www.iuniverse.com
844-349-9409

Because of the dynamic nature of the Internet, any web addresses or links contained in this book may have changed since publication and may no longer be valid. The views expressed in this work are solely those of the author and do not necessarily reflect the views of the publisher, and the publisher hereby disclaims any responsibility for them.

Any people depicted in stock imagery provided by Getty Images are models, and such images are being used for illustrative purposes only. Certain stock imagery © Getty Images.

ISBN: 978-1-6632-1558-1 (sc)
ISBN: 978-1-6632-1559-8 (e)

Print information available on the last page.

iUniverse rev. date: 01/21/2021

THE ART OF COMMERCIAL DRUMMING

How to develop a solid groove and become a
POCKET DRUMMER

ROBERT SHIPLEY

iUniverse

Rhythm Patterns
Part 1

4

Rhythm Patterns
Part 2

Rhythm Patterns
Part 3

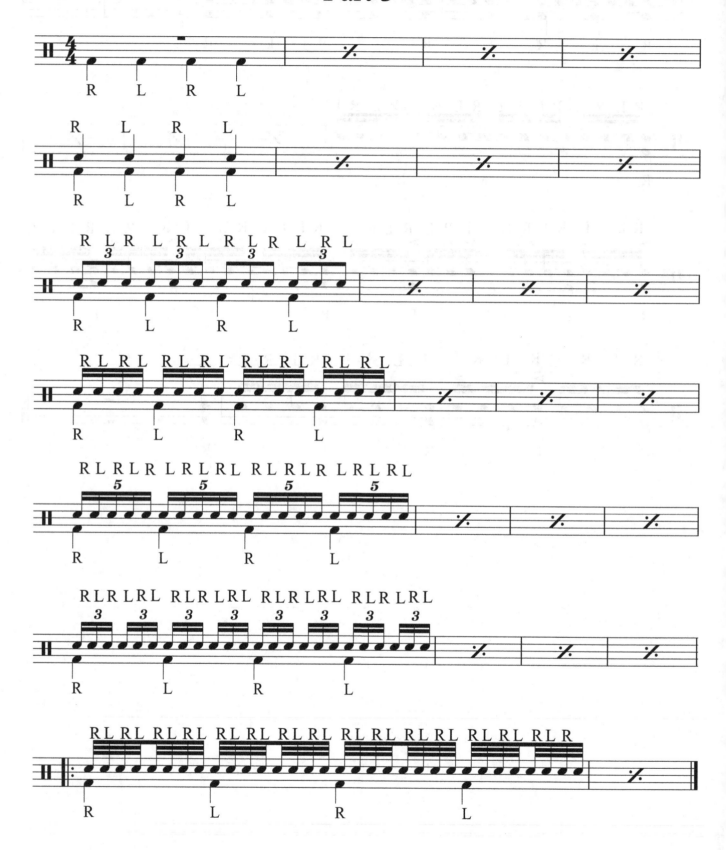

POCKET DRUMMING
Notation Key

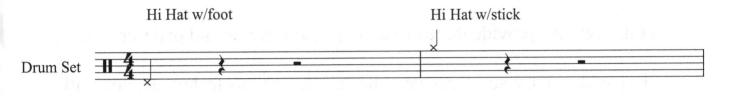

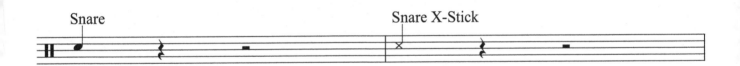

SYSTEMS AND PATTERNS

In this section I provide three systems. These systems and patterns will

help you develop a solid groove. After mastering this technique, you will

be a **POCKET DRUMMER**

Memorize each system.

Play the system while reading the various bass drum patterns.

POCKET DRUMMING
Systems

System #1

Drum Set

System #2

System #3

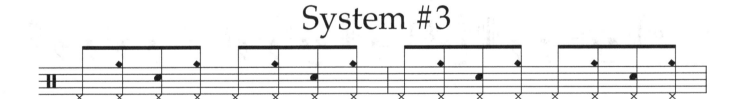

ROCK DOUBLE BASS DRUM

We will begin this exercise with the basic building blocks.
If 80 beats per minute are difficult. Slow the metronome to find your comfort zone.
Remember, the best way to play fast is to start SLOW.

This eight note cymbal pattern will be played on the Ride cymbal with the right hand.
This eight note bass drum pattern will be played with the right foot.

After you are comfortable with the previous pattern.
Let's add the snare drum on 2 & 4. Played with the left hand.

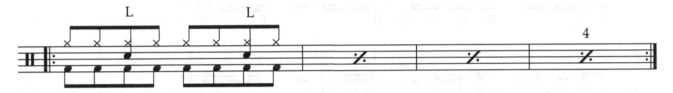

After you are comfortable with the previous pattern.
Let's create a sixteenth note bass drum pattern by playing the left foot after every right foot stroke.

The previous pattern will become our two bar ostinato.
This two bar ostinato will be followed by various two bar patterns.
Here is an example:

14

SINGLES

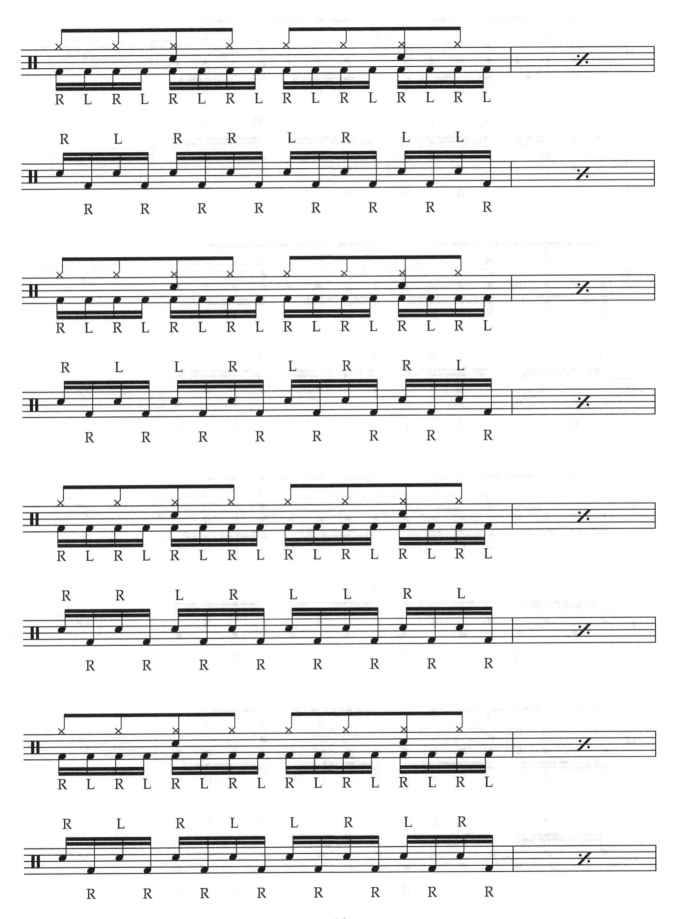

17

R L R L R L R L R L R L R L R L

R   R   R   R   L   L   L   L

R   R   R   R   R   R   R   R

DOUBLES

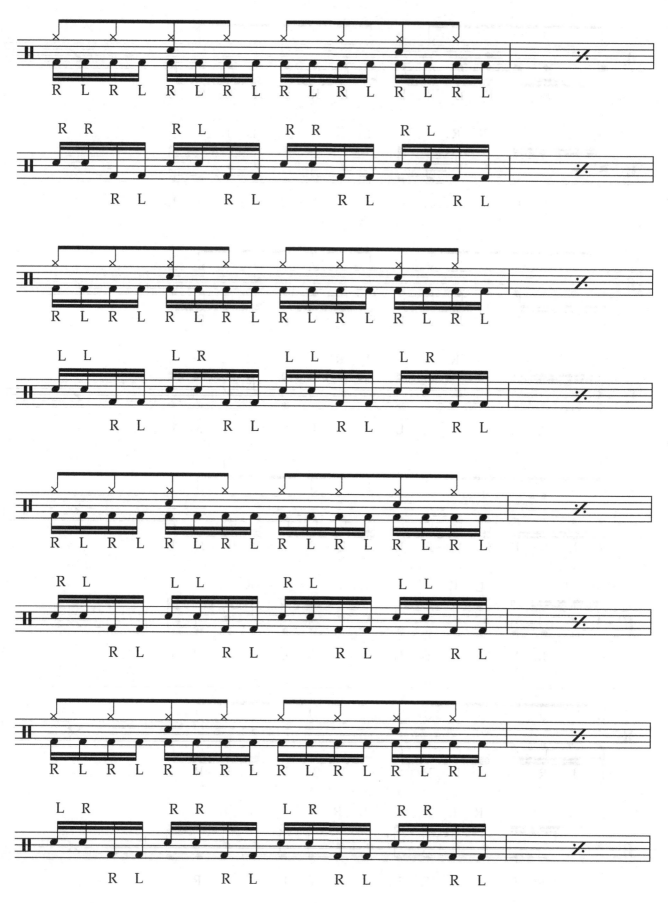

21

TRIPLETS

23

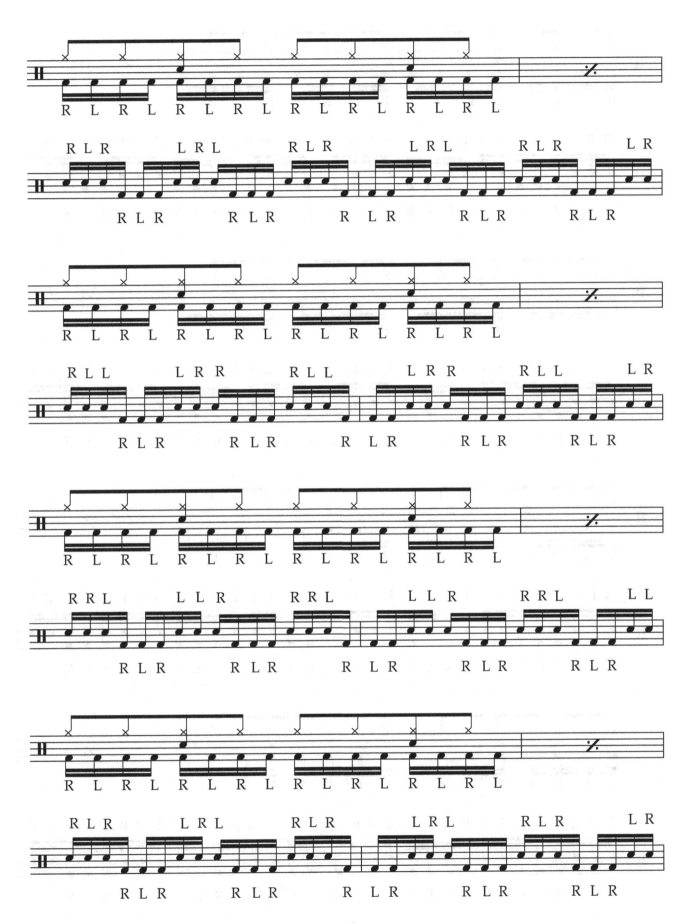

24

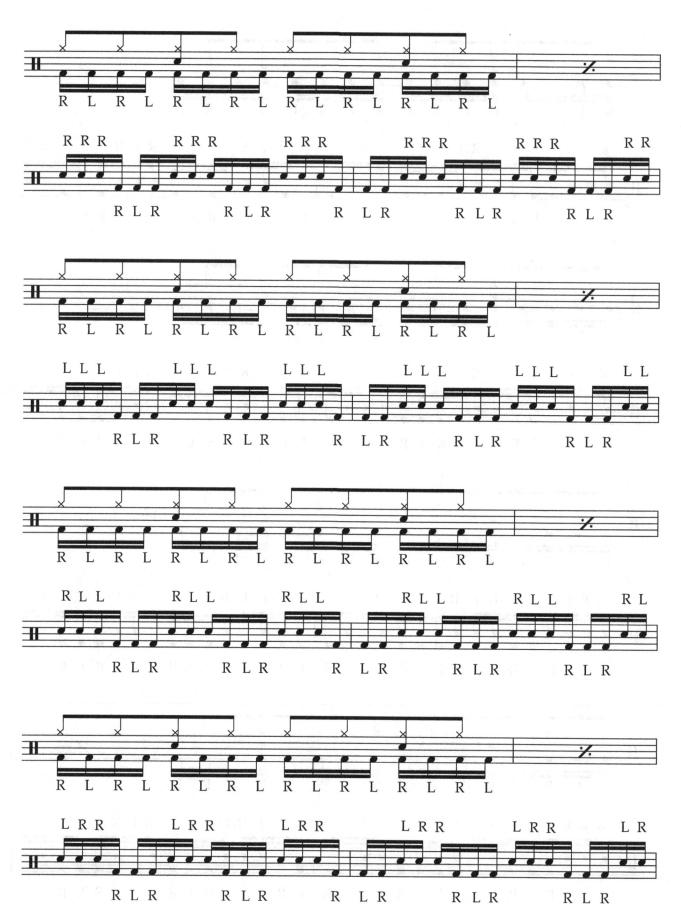

25

R L R L R L R L R L R L R L R L

R R R   L L L   R R R   L L L   R R R   L L

R L R   R L R   R L R   R L R   R L R

QUADRUPLES

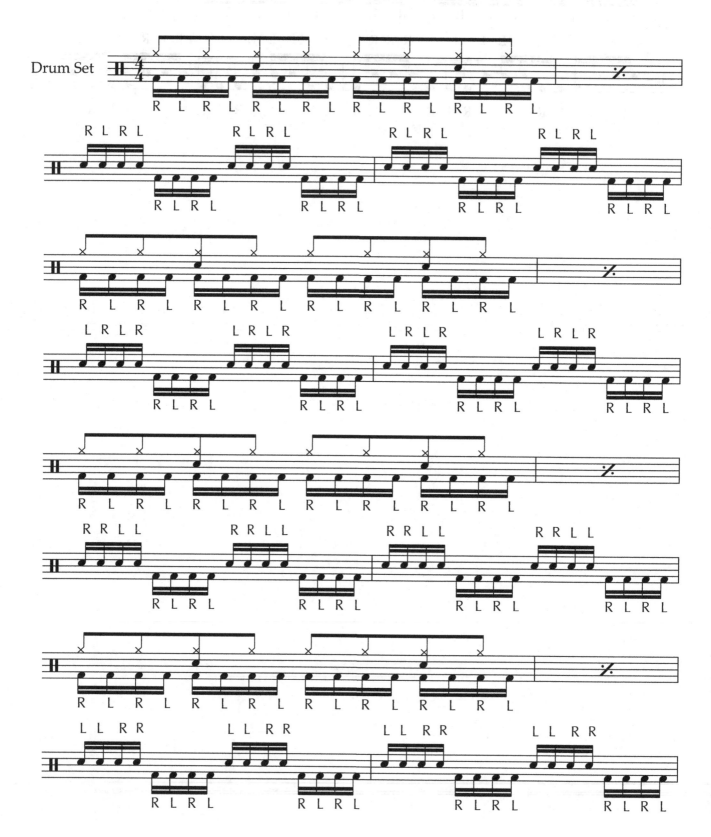

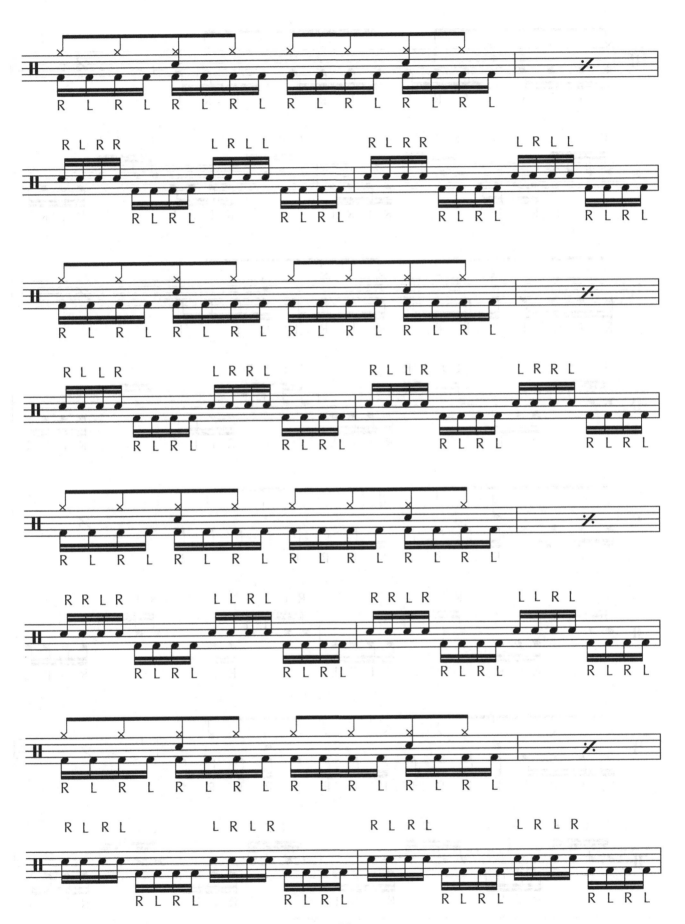

28

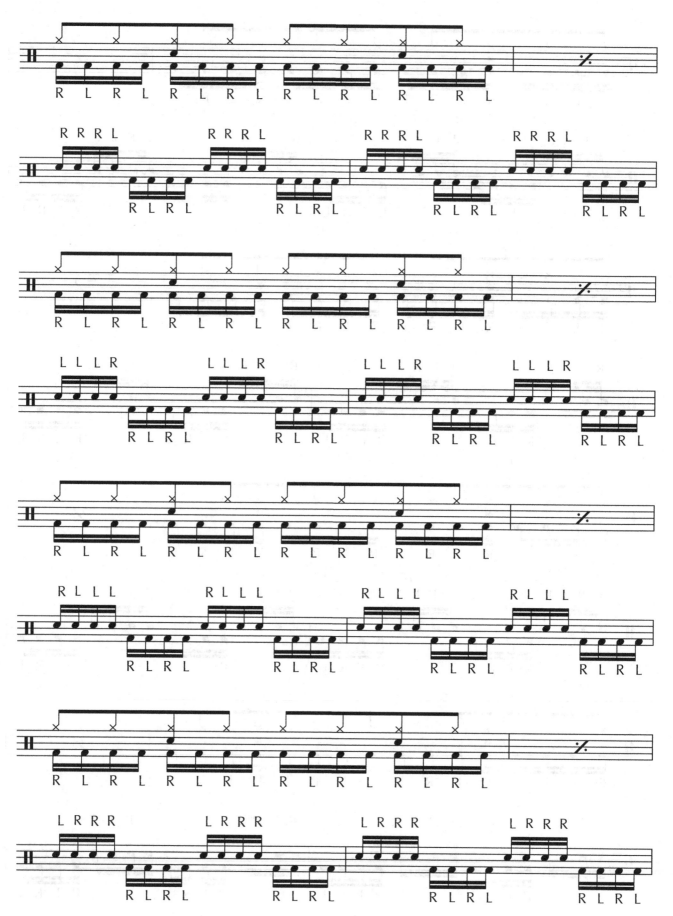

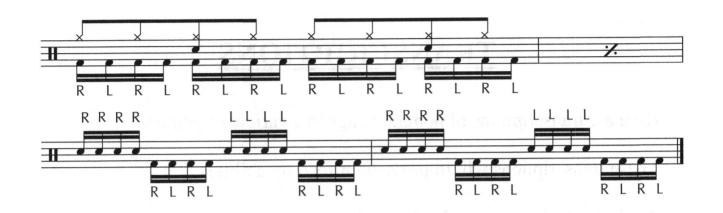

TRANSCRIPTIONS

Here are transcriptions of popular songs in a variety of genres.

These transcriptions will improve your reading abilities.

Apply the techniques you've learned for developing a solid groove while

playing these charts and you'll be well on your way to being a

POCKET DRUMMER.

24K MAGIC

BRUNO MARS

Transcribed by
Robert Shipley

2

SWEET HOME ALABAMA
LYNYRD SKYNYRD

Transcribed by
Robert Shipley

35

UPTOWN FUNK

MARK RONSON feat. BRUNO MARS

Transcribed by
Robert Shipley

2

4

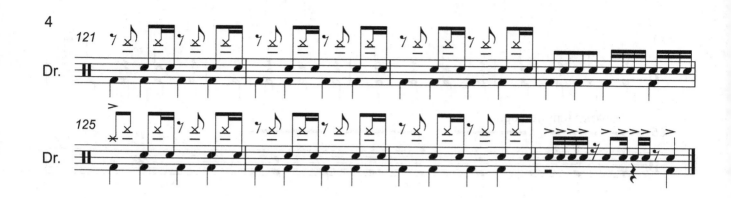

LIVIN LA VIDA LOCA
RICKY MARTIN

Transcribed by
Robert Shipley

42

2

43

ARE YOU GONNA GO MY WAY

LENNY KRAVITZ

Transcribed by
Robert Shipley

Crash Ride

To Slightly Open HiHat

Verse

WANNABE
SPICE GIRLS

Transcribed by
Robert Shipley

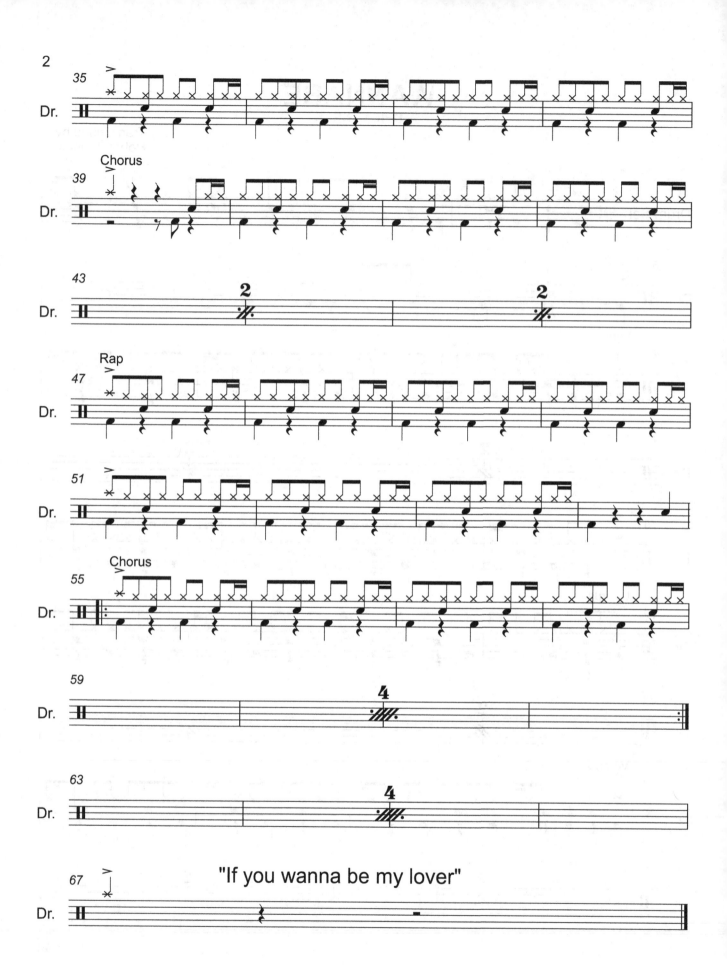

BABY ONE MORE TIME

Transcribed by
Robert Shipley

2

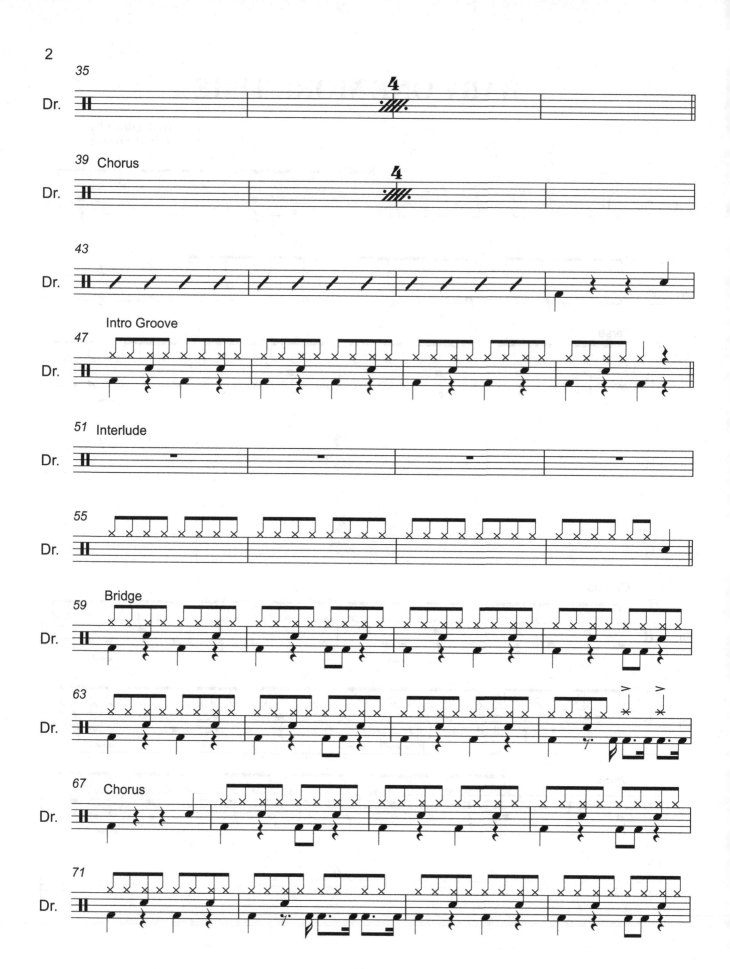

"Hit me baby one more time"

BILLY JEAN

Transcribed by
Robert Shipley

JUST WHAT I NEEDED

Transcribed by
Robert Shipley

2

Printed in the United States
By Bookmasters